# The G.U.D. Life:

# We Are Chosen

Stories Anthologized By:

***Shervondaline Sims Breedlove***

Visionary Anthologist

ISBN: 978-0-57899244-0-2


www.brdpublications.com

# *Dedication*

We dedicate this book to our babies, who we were so excited
to teach about Living, Learning, Laughing, and Loving.

Ironically, they have taught us more than we could have ever imagined
about Faith, Hope, Trust, and Love.

# Contents

# *Share Your G.U.D.® Thoughts With Us*

**We would love to hear your feedback, reactions, and thoughts on the stories in this book. Please let us know which stories were your favorites and how they positively affected and impacted you.**

**Please connect with us for future books in our series at:**
**www.thegudlifeuniversal.com**

**We hope you enjoy reading this book as much as we enjoyed sharing our G.U.D.® journeys and testimonies with you.**

# Foreword

Have you ever been so tired that you could not seem to think straight? Not the physical tiredness that comes just from the fun of getting older. I am speaking of the mental aspect - the type that causes you to forget why you walked into a room. The tiredness that causes you to put the car keys in the refrigerator accidentally. That form of tiredness when you are talking on your cell phone and looking for it at the same time or could not find the glasses you had on your head while you were looking for them for thirty minutes.

In society, much is centered on children and adults who have been diagnosed with Autism, Special Needs, and other disabilities. However, I feel it is vital to acknowledge the mothers, grandmothers, siblings, caregivers, and educators who play a critical role in the lives of those children and individuals impacted by these various conditions. Some of you may feel overwhelmed, overlooked, or even overworked. Please know that God does not give you any more than you can handle. He intervenes on your behalf to help you handle your assignment from Him.

Being mothers, grandmothers, siblings, caregivers, and educators might seem like thankless jobs, but it is undeniable that the care you deliver is invaluable. Caring for someone else demonstrates your love and commitment to that individual. It often feels like you are constantly doing something for someone else every day. Then just at the moment when it feels like too much, you get an "I love you!" or "You are the best teacher ever!" and instantly, it makes all your hard work worth it. When you care for or educate a child with Autism or Special Needs, the job is even more complex. Sadly, many people do not understand all that is entailed.

Only mothers of Autistic and Special Needs children know and understand what it feels like to be stared at in the grocery store or a public setting while their child is having a meltdown or for others to judge them thinking that their child is simply misbehaving or unruly. All mothers have ups and downs with their children. Nevertheless, when a mother's child has Autism, Special Needs, or disabilities, sometimes there are many more downs than ups. After putting your child to bed, you have a bigger job which is advocating for your child. You must make sure that they are prepared for their routine day in and day out. I want Autism and Special Needs moms to always remember that they have a Comforter who is with them. Isaiah 41:10 NKJV reads, "Fear not, for I am with you; Be not dismayed, for I am your God. I will strengthen you, Yes, I will help you, I will uphold you with My righteous right hand".

Although caring for yourself should be a necessity, self-care is sometimes not a priority on your to-do list or maybe even neglected altogether when caring for someone else. Autism and Special Needs moms should balance caring for their spiritual, physical, mental, and emotional health as they serve and care for others. You can do this by practicing self-care behavior. Some of you may feel like implementing self-care in your health and well-being regimen is selfish. It may make you feel guilty, or you may think that self-care is not necessary. However, it is vital to take some time out for yourself. Take care of your mental, physical, emotional, and spiritual health. When you develop and maintain these routines, you are equipped to help others efficiently and effectively. Please know that your mental health matters. You are loved and appreciated even though your loved ones or students may not be able to tell you personally.

One of the most important things that you can do for yourself is to take care of yourself. Self-care is about recharging, renewing, relaxing, and refreshing our souls, minds, bodies, and spirits. Self-care is treating yourself with care, consideration, compassion, and love. Attend to your own mental health needs, pray and meditate, build your support system, accept help when needed, take time to participate in some pleasurable nurturing activity, exercise, and get proper sleep and nutrition.

No matter what you decide to do to practice self-care, it is essential to remember God loves you and He cares for you, so begin with God and end with God.

— Dr. Gayberyl L. Wesley

**Dr. Gayberyl L. Wesley is from Monroe, Louisiana.** She is credentialed as a Licensed Master Social Worker and has eleven years of Social Work practice. As a Grambling State University Assistant Professor, she presently teaches undergraduate and graduate levels through face-to-face and virtual learning. Her primary teaching instruction includes Human Behavior and the Social Environment, Substance Abuse Issues in Social Work Practice, Assessment and Diagnostic Systems, Child Welfare, and Writing for Professional Social Workers. Dr. Wesley is the GSU Master of Social Work Admissions Coordinator, serves on the GSU Faculty Senate, and mentors graduate students in capstone writing.

Dr. Wesley has a certification in Leadership from Rhema Leadership Institute. She achieved two Bachelor's degrees. The first is in Entrepreneurship and Marketing from the University of Louisiana at Monroe and the second is in Theology and Religious

Studies from Hope Bible Institute. She obtained a Master's degree in Social Work from Grambling State University. She earned a Doctoral degree in Social Work from Capella University. Her dissertation titled "Ameliorating Compassion Fatigue with Family Caregivers: An Appreciative Inquiry" was published by ProQuest in 2016. This publication examined the quality of life and well-being of family caregivers of persons with long-term health conditions. It fostered the need for caregivers to practice self-care. Dr. Wesley's current research focuses primarily on student retention in higher education, substance use, and mental health disorders. She is currently earning a Ph.D. in Education with a specialization in Higher Education, Leadership, and Policy from Walden University.

In addition to her professional responsibilities and roles, she is a member of the Association of Black Social Workers, an Assistant Treasurer and Executive Member of the Monroe/Ouachita Parish NAACP Chapter, a member of St. Luke Baptist Church of Alto, Louisiana, and a proud member of Sigma Gamma Rho Sorority, Inc. She also is a member of numerous other professional and civic organizations.

# *Introduction*

Can you think of any situation when a lunch break is justifiably more important than a human life? My brother, Kenneth Dewayne Harris, was born on December 4, 1959. Our family lovingly calls him "Wayne." His was an unusual birth. My mother informed her obstetrician that she was already in labor with Wayne just before he was born. Therefore, he knew that my mother was close to giving birth. However, he told my mom that he was going to take his lunch break. He advised that if the baby came, it would have to birth itself or wait until he got back from lunch. During his break, my mother's birthing process began. Due to complications from lack of enough oxygen to his brain, Wayne was born mentally disabled. Unfortunately, it was not known to my mother at that time.

About five years later, it was time for Wayne to start school, kindergarten, to be exact. Before Wayne began school, he was normal to my sister and me. She was six years old, and I was seven years old. Although we knew Wayne was a little *different*, we thought it was due to him being younger than us. Then, while I was in the second grade, Wayne started attending our elementary school. This milestone is when it became apparent that Wayne was much *different* from anybody in our school.

On many days, Wayne's teacher would pull me out of my class to come and settle Wayne down. He would be fighting and biting the other children who were making fun of him because they knew he was *different. In retaliation,* Wayne would take their milk and cookies from them. Wayne hated taking naps, so he would stay awake and play during nap time. His teacher would often rely on me to calm him down. You see, at home, Wayne was free to be himself with very few restrictions, but at school, there were rules. This situation lasted a few weeks, maybe even months, until Wayne was expelled from our school. He seriously bit and injured another student. In addition to that, his destructiveness was too disruptive to the classroom and his classmates. As a result, my parents found a different school for Wayne with other kids similar to him.

Over the years, I watched my mother's challenges raising Wayne into adulthood. Our mother was the perfect mom for raising Wayne, especially after she became a single parent. Getting Wayne to and from doctor appointments entailed countless physical struggles for my mother. Yet, I observed her exceptional characteristics and unique qualities as a strong woman until the day she went to Heaven. She accepted the fact that she would spend her entire adult life taking care of Wayne. She understood that he would never marry, leave home, have a career, or become self-sufficient. Although she was sometimes exhausted, she believed that God had chosen her for this special assignment. My mother often voiced it to me and everyone else.

Consequently, when my daughter, her granddaughter, gave birth to her great-grandson, who was born with vision impairment and Autism, my mom was able to help and support my daughter tremendously. Furthermore, my mother was instrumental in helping my daughter understand the gift God had given her in her son. Thus, we are a marvelously blessed family with God's special anointing upon us to graciously deal with the hand we have been dealt.

Before my grandson came into our lives, I knew very little about Autism. I had only encountered people with the condition on a few occasions. However, after receiving his diagnosis and observing him, I became highly interested in this neurological developmental disability.

While lying on his back during playtime, I noticed that he was laughing, but his eyes were not following me. I cannot remember if I asked my daughter about my concerns at the time. I did not know if she had also noticed that her firstborn seemed a little *different*. Nonetheless, we were so glad to have him in our lives and totally in love with him that we either overlooked what we both or all might have suspected but were too enamored with our two-month-old bundle of joy to address.

A few months later, we received a call from our daughter and heard the news. While processing the fearful emotions in her voice and the uncertainty of what was going on with her beloved baby, I immediately went into positive affirmations. I spoke The Word into my daughter's life to assure her that everything would be all right with Denym.

God did not make a mistake when He chose her to be the mother of this gifted baby boy or my mother to be Wayne's caregiver. I am a firm believer that mothers who give birth to babies and raise children who are diagnosed with Autism, Special Needs, and other disabilities are granted an exceptional amount of God's Grace. Wayne and Denym have only brought joy and sunshine into our lives.

Summarily, I want to say to all of you who have a child, grandchild, relative, loved one, student, neighbor, or church member who has Autism, Special Needs, or any other condition, please understand that God remarkably gifts these children to shine in whichever capacity He chooses in this life to glorify Him. So, count it as an honor to have this unique individual in your life.

— Apostle Lee T. Harris, Jr.

**Apostle Lee T. Harris, Jr.** was born in Monroe, Louisiana. His parents moved him and his two siblings to California when he was two years old. He lived there for thirty-nine years until he, his wife Davida, and four of their children relocated to Memphis, Tennessee, where they still reside today.

He received Jesus Christ on Thanksgiving night in 1984. God called him to preach the Gospel shortly after accepting Christ. Subsequently, he returned to his birthplace and preached his first sermon in Monroe, Louisiana in 1986.

Apostle Harris and his wife pastored the Dramatic Grace & Faith Church for eighteen years. Together, they also started an international ministry, Word Of Impact Global Ministry, which they still run today. He has preached in several countries around the world, including South Africa, South Korea, Hong Kong,

London, UK, Germany, New Zealand, Australia, Canada, Bahamas, Mexico, and the Philippines.

Apostle Harris operates in a dynamic prophetic anointing gift upon his life through the leading of the Holy Spirit. He is still currently preaching the Gospel throughout the United States as well internationally. Apostle Harris authored a book to inspire and motivate women titled "Woman of God, From Nowhere to Everywhere."

Apostle Lee and his wife, Davida have three sons, five daughters, and sixteen grandchildren.

# *Tips For A G.U.D. Life*

1. **Think G.U.D. Thoughts**
2. **Speak G.U.D. Words**
3. **Do G.U.D. Deeds**
4. **Expect G.U.D. Things**
5. **Be Grateful For Your G.U.D. Blessings**

# *"Denym: Like The Jeans"*

*by*

***Leticia A. Harris***

When God elects you to care for one of His Special Needs children, you accept it and enter into a "new world" that is no longer your own. A different world that we all know exists, but we never imagine being a part of it. So how does one truly prepare for a new world? First, you put on The Whole Armor of God because it is an enigmatic world that no one actually thinks about until it is right in front of you. You must wear your Armor nights, days, weekends, and holidays as this child becomes your world, full of bewildering and precious moments. Also grip the importance of the Helmet of Salvation, as the enemy will try to take your mind and have you blaming yourself for your child's disability, when in fact, God has appointed you an ultra-premium gift that all are not worthy to receive. This sacred gift may, in fact, first coincide with hurt and despair, but then comes strength and comfort followed by unspeakable joy.

On a sunny California winter day {literally}, born healthy and hungry at forty-one weeks, Denym, aka Bubba, hit the scene. The whole family was excited about Denym, especially his *"Granny-Granny."* She would look after him while I worked. She would be holding him when I left and still holding him when I would return. They created a special bond very early on.

At six months, Denym was diagnosed with Optic Nerve Hypoplasia {Visually Impaired/Legally Blind}, Ataxia Cerebral Palsy, growth hormone deficiencies, and developmental delays. As the doctor stood there reading all his findings, I remember thinking, *"What in the world does all this mean? Does he know that I have no idea what he is saying?"* Then he asks, *"Any questions?"* I replied, *"No."*, knowing full well, I had not one stinking clue what any of what he said meant. Once the doctor walked out, I instantly called my Granny in devastation. Within the same hour, she was there. She told me that she just had to come to the hospital to hold *her* Bubba.

There was *one* word the doctor said that I *thought* I knew, *"blind."* Yet, I was blind to the *true* meaning. Like me, you heard the word and might have assumed that my son was *"in the dark"* blind. That is not the case. In fact, there are different variations of blindness. By Denym being only six months when diagnosed, we would have to wait until he got older to know what he could and could not see. However, we *knew* that he certainly was not completely blind. He was legally blind and visually impaired.

A few months after Denym's diagnosis, he began receiving in-home therapy to motivate him to sit up by utilizing different objects and toys to see which ones would stimulate him. One day his therapist, Cristal, brought a Little Tikes® Four-Key Piano with lights. It was simply music to Bubba's ears! He loved banging his delicate little hands on that piano. Eventually, it was the tool that initiated his crawling phase. Shortly after that, the therapist arrived with a bigger Little Tikes® Piano to help encourage Bubba to stand. It lit up, too! Ohhh, Denym was elated in his own one-year-old delightful way. It ultimately inspired him to pull himself up and stand. From then on, Denym's little piano traveled everywhere we went. My Granny used to say, *"I bet you he is gonna teach himself how to really play that thing one day."*

It was not until ***years*** later that I was informed that my son was indeed Autistic and then everything made sense. It explained why he would flip out if someone accidentally shut the lights off or if a door slammed. He had separation attacks when I would leave. He would *cry* nonstop for *hours*! It *all* made sense. His frame of mind is in a totally different dimension. I had to first learn from him, then know what would and would not work when communicating and understanding Denym. I learned that when you tell Denym you are going to do something, you better mean it! For example, if you said that he would get ice cream at 2:00, then at 1:59, somebody better be asking him what flavor he wants, or else he would create a stink, and everyone would smell it! Some think he is spoiled or rotten, but it is simply a matter of being mindful of what you say to him. He comes with expectations. The old phrase, *"Say what you mean and* mean what you say!" perfectly describes the lesson to learn on how to successfully understand and deal with Bubba.

We all genuinely know that every child is a gift from God. Therefore, to be blessed with a Special Needs child, two more children, and accede single parenthood, ooh wee Lord, your gifts prove that You have a sense of humor! At one point, all three children were still in diapers. They all got a stomach bug. After the thirtieth diaper change in one day, I threw a soiled diaper across the room in overwhelming defeat. I quickly thought, *"What have I done? Please do not explode upon impact! Jesus, be a fence around that pamper as it glides through the air or I will jump off my second-story balcony!"*

'Diaper Duty' had overtaken me that day, but thank God for a safe landing. The Lord knew my heart, understood my heartache, and cared about my frustration. Potty Training sat on the back burner because it was easier for me to just change him instead of physically attacking the challenge of toilet learning with a child whose comprehension was just different. Honestly, potty training in general was the most avoided battle for me. There was already so much in life to sort through that "pee-pee and boo-boo" in the pot was not another hurdle that I cared to face. Not to mention the fact that I have a bathroom phobia and nearly puked just typing those words. Should I be ashamed that Denym was still in diapers until he was seven or eight years old? Maybe, but I just did not have it in me. I just could not carry out potty training for any of my children. It took two extraordinary individuals to take that load off my hands, and I will forever appreciate it.

My time had become so divided and compartmentalized that it caused me to slip into a medicated depression. I would stay up all night, sleep while kids were at school, and work in between. I always knew God was near because I kept him close by keeping a song of praise in my heart, as my stepmother suggested. Some memories are just too painful. A few of the wounds are still only scabbed. Peel back that scab, and one will still bleed. Yet, you learn to live. Live while hurt. Live while scarred. Live while confused. Live while frustrated. Live while feeling neglected and unloved. Live when you do not know what you are doing. Live. Live and continue to worship because Jesus says, *"It will not last always."* So, you get up the next day and the next day. That was me in some of Denym's early years. It was not only because of him, but having a child with Special Needs, two other small children, working full-time, the kids' absent father, my grandmother's sudden death, and then going to school at night: the phrase "a lot" was an understatement. Drowning, but still afloat. Every bill and every meal fell on my head. Every doctor's appointment, every WIC appointment, every DHS appointment, every dentist appointment, every IEP meeting, every grocery store run, every Chuck-E Cheese playdate, every Incredible Pizza outing, every first day: it all took a piece of me. Not only did I learn how to carry the weight, but I figured out how to balance the load too!

Denym's siblings, especially his little brother Dylon, who is fourteen months younger, took on more than any child should have had to. He is truly his brother's keeper. At two years old, I taught him how to strap three-year-old Bubba into his car seat. On our battlefield, we all had more roles than an average household had. It caused me to pick and choose battles every day. Everything became a battlefield. And yes, of course, I got my King Jesus on the battlefield with me, but this ole flesh we live in waivers at times.

When Denym was six or seven years old, we were enduring very trying times. My aunt, his great aunt, discovered that Denym actually had taught himself to play the piano. Sometimes, he was really cool with it! He played with one hand while lying on his back. We were amazed that he was playing the piano in real life. He began playing at school assemblies and other school district functions. Denym's music playing ranged from the Star-Spangled Banner to Mozart to Break Every Chain to Tupac's California Love. He is an ultra- premium gift indeed. To see crowds of people cheering him on made my heart so proud. Sometimes he would need to know a little incentive was involved before his performance began. Once he was on stage at the Hilton in Memphis, getting ready to play, and as he sits down at the piano, he says into the mic, *"Mom, you gonna get me pancakes?"* The crowd starts laughing. I shout back, *"Yes, Bubba!"* and he carries on like planned. Say what you mean and mean what you say, ok.

*Denym, like the jeans,* is resilient, strong, faithful, and everyone loves him. I can guarantee anyone who has ever met him will never forget Denym, as he makes a genuine everlasting impression.

On countless occasions, I find myself just watching Bubba play and laugh to himself. He has pure joy in his heart. And to see God's pure joy first hand, how could one not appreciate every little thing in life? Denym is currently eighteen years old and will be graduating with his brother in 2022. We do not know what the next part of our journey will entail. However, I have learned to embrace struggles and trials since I know in my heart that my God is in the midst of it all.

Now, that does not mean I know how to deal with everything thrown my way, but there is a clear understanding that I ***can*** do all things through Christ who strengthens me. {Philippians 4:13} My Lord Jesus indeed saw me, He held me, He kept my head on straight when pleading insanity certainly would have applied. But God! Some days are still more challenging than others. They require patience, believing in the grace of God, and knowing that His mighty hand is upon us. Nevertheless, I am content since I know: if He brings me to it, He will bring me through it.

> ***"You are my refuge and my shield; your word is my source of hope."*** ***Psalm 119:114 NLT***

**Leticia Adeah Harris** was born and bred in Riverside, California. At twenty-four years old, she decided to leave "home" and move to Memphis, Tennessee. Some of her family members had previously moved there. While living in Memphis, she went back to culinary school and graduated Magna Cum Laude from LeCole Culinaire in 2010. Graduation was a profoundly proud day, seeing her children, watching her walk across the stage. Thanks to Memphis, Leticia grew, learned, became the woman she is today. However, she has no desire to return.

After almost ten years in Tennessee, she had another urge to move away. So, in 2014, she packed up and moved her three children to Mesa, Arizona, where they currently reside. She works as a Pastry Chef. It is through God's grace and anointing that she has become a true Chef at heart. One day, Leticia hopes to work for herself full-time again in the future. She has always been her children's advocate and they know it. With all three children in high school now, she sees the light at the end of the tunnel ~ although her job as a mom will never end.

**Connect with Leticia**
Email: lahrris@gmail.com

# "Dear Gabby,"

*by*

***Stephanie B. Morris***

*Dear Gabby,*

***Gabrielle Alexis Butler***
***Birthdate: January 26, 1993***
***Time: 5:57 PM***
***Weight: 6 lbs. 15 1/2 ounces 18 1/4 inches long***
***Location: Mississippi Baptist Medical Center ~ Jackson, Mississippi***

The history of the day you were born was documented by the hospital where I gave birth to you. Life will bring you many delightful adventures! You were destined to be a part of the history of our country and our world! A record of what the world around you was like on your birthday has been documented for you and your family! Cherish the history of your special day. It is the day you began your journey into life!

Your birth situation was plagued by circumstances that required Doctor Paul Rice to perform an emergency C-section instead of the natural birth I had planned. I was given an epidural to ensure I would not feel anything. Yet, I still felt the pressure when he pulled you out of my belly. My mother said you were born with your eyes wide open because she was right there waiting on you to make your grand entrance! She decided to put on the scrubs even though she always said she would never wear any pants. However, she did on that special day ~ just for you! According to the doctor, you were in the headfirst position trying to descend, but the umbilical cord was wrapped around your neck. Your grandmother shared how there was also a knot in the cord as big as the doctor's fist. Your heart rate continued to drop, but God knew I would need you to keep fighting until you arrived here! God already predestined an excellent purpose for your life.

I could hear the nurses discussing everything about you. How I wanted to breastfeed, but you would not latch on. Despite all the obstacles in your way, you still fought to get here! You are a true fighter. I thank God that He allowed you to be born and live! Growing up was a little difficult for you with the early seizures, but the enemy could not defeat you! You kept striving. You were reaching all the milestones set for a child your age. Even though you are non-ambulatory and non-verbal, you are a true blessing to our family and me! You prolonged your grandmother's and grandfather's lives while they were alive. Now, you are extending mine too!

While you were growing up, I had lots of help with you from my parents, brothers, their families, and our friends. They all assisted with getting you back and forth to your appointments, which were many at that time. During your early years, I learned about a doctor by the name of Doctor Veda Vettakikora. He was a seizure disorder specialist. He diagnosed your seizure activity at the University of Mississippi Medical Center {UMMC}. Starting at three months old, Doctor Veda prescribed a cocktail of medicines for you to take. However, we had to learn the side effects of some of the medicine. One of the medications, Phenobarbital, was habit- forming. It irritated your stomach. You had an adverse reaction. Instead, we began using another group of medicines. The combination of Tegretol and Keppra controlled your seizures much better than the first medication which caused abdominal problems.

The Willowood Development Center is the elementary school you attended with other children who also had Special Needs. While there, you received evaluation after evaluation. The most meaningful evaluation results were the ones that confirmed you were Developmentally Delayed. Next, I found out about McCloud Elementary. It was a public school near us that also accepted children with Special Needs. I enrolled you there. After McCloud, you attended North Jackson Elementary with the Special Needs class. You reconnected with some classmates from Willowood Development Center. In January 2011, you joined the Hudspeth Regional Development Center Family. There you received a comprehensive evaluation. Your hearing and vision evaluations were completed to determine your standing in these areas. At Hudspeth, you grew and had several beneficial experiences! One of your future benefits is having the opportunity to utilize the

Medicaid Waiver Program offered through Hudspeth Regional. As a former resident of Hudspeth Regional Center and Hollyhouse Cottage, you are now in your own house, which is a courtesy to the Medicaid Waiver Program participants. The Medicaid Waiver Program services are offered by The Oxford Home Health Care Agency of Jackson, Mississippi. Currently, your home is only about five minutes away from my house. I am so thankful for that because it is unlike the fifteen miles from my house to Hudspeth Center that I used to drive.

Dr. Veda, your Pediatric Neurologist, once told me that someone with your diagnosis would not live a productive life. However, you have defied the odds and lived past your predicted age limit of two years old. Now, you are twenty- eight years old! It makes me so proud to say you have not had another seizure since you have been on Keppra! Since you are non-verbal and non-ambulatory, I had to teach you the difference between your needs and your wants.

I thank the Lord for all the marvelous things He has done! I am grateful for you being alive. God only knows how much I thank Him for giving you to me! I praise Him for your life right now! I am so appreciative of the opportunities you received at the Hudspeth Regional Center. You enjoyed prom activities while you were there. You won Little Miss Hudspeth Center, and you were crowned from 2013-2014. The class of 2014 was blessed and privileged to have you as a graduate from the C. B. Noblin School at the Hudspeth Regional Center.

You are often out in the community enjoying yourself and doing more now that you are on your own, which is a perfect thing! This is all that I ever wanted for you! Furthermore, I want your quality of life to be greater than mine. More so, I even want you to attend the Mississippi State Fair more than me!

Now, I will end this letter because I could go on and on about the many miraculous things God has done for you! However, I want you to know that I will always be your biggest cheerleader, I will always be your confidant, and I will always be proud of you. I will love you unconditionally forever because I will always be your mother!

Sincerely,
Your Mother

***"Beloved, I pray that you may prosper in all things and be in good health, just as your soul prospers."***
***3 John 2 NKJV***

**Evangelist Missionary Stephanie Evonne Butler Morris** is the first of three children born to the Late Elder Levi Butler and the Late Missionary Charlene Russell-Butler of Jackson, Mississippi. She is a very active member of the House of Prayer Church of God in Christ in Pearl, Mississippi. Elder Willie Lee Scott is her Pastor and District Missionary Nancee Scott is her District Missionary. She is an active member of her district and serves her jurisdiction as the Public Relations/Special Projects Director for the Women's Department under Mother Frankie Davis-Murray and Bishop Daniel T. Littleton of Mississippi Southern First Ecclesiastical Jurisdiction Church of God in Christ.

The 'apple of her eye' is her beautiful daughter, Gabrielle Alexis, affectionately known as *"Gabby"* to whom she is a devoted mother. As a part of her dedication to Gabby and persons with Special Needs, Missionary Morris currently hosts a special gospel supper club fund-raising event called *"PRAISES: The Ultimate Christian Experience."* The purpose of this event is to showcase the many special talents of the clients of Hudspeth Regional Center. A few of her national artist friends, such as Mr. Harvey Watkins, Jr. and The Canton Spirituals, Mr. Stan Jones, and Ms. Vicki Yohe, add a touch of flavor to the guest list! Stephanie was recently appointed as President of the Friends of Hudspeth Center non-profit organization. She and the association are dedicated to providing support to the State-operated center.

As an original charter member of the Mississippi Mass Choir since May 6, 1988, Missionary Morris has traveled extensively across the United States and Overseas with the choir giving God praise through song.

Stephanie is a 1985 Dean's List graduate from the University of Southern Mississippi in Accounting. She retired from the State of Mississippi Development Authority, as an Economic Development Senior Finance Manager. In that role, she assisted small, minority, and women-owned businesses in business startup and receiving finance assistance. Missionary Morris is also very active in her community and in her own small business venture, SEBGAB Productions. Her production company includes special events coordination, gospel music booking, promotions, and management. SEBGAB also offers accounting services and business financing.

Most of all, she would like for you to know that her personal testimony is Romans 8:37-39 which says, *"Nay, in all these things we are more than conquerors through Him that loved us."* She says, *"For I am persuaded, that neither life, nor death, nor angels, nor principalities, nor powers, nor things present, nor things to come; nor height, nor depth, nor any other creature, shall be able to separate me from the love of God, which is in Christ Jesus our Lord."*

**Connect with Stephanie**

Email: stephaniebutler2693@gmail.com

# "Smoking Gun"

*by*
***Lelia D. Henderson***

Wow, I never would have imagined that I would become a single mom raising two sons alone. I can still remember when I transferred to Grambling State University from the University of Arkansas Pine Bluff. I met a young mother with a small son who had an Autism diagnosis. I loved me some him. I always told her that I admired how strong she was as I watched her raise her son alone. Who would have thought I would later become a parent of a child with an Autism diagnosis?

My youngest son, Kory, was diagnosed with Autism at the age of six. Through my mother's intuition, I always knew there was something different and unique about Kory. My oldest son, P.J., started walking between ten and eleven months. He began speaking words and saying phrases at this age as well.

At twelve months, I noticed that Kory was not walking. Although he was a chunky baby, he was still trying to pull up. He was born six weeks early, weighing 8 pounds and 9 ounces. During my pregnancy, my obstetrician repeatedly told me that my baby would be significantly larger than average at birth. I was admitted into the hospital for three months and required to have weekly ultrasounds. I was released from the hospital, but I ended up going into pre-term labor within three weeks. Since Kory was not walking at twelve months old, I took him to see our pediatrician. The doctor listened to my concerns, we discussed his options, and he prescribed various therapies immediately. Kory received approval for speech, physical, and occupational therapies. At one point, we were going to thirty-six appointments each month ~ which is two or three per day. Kory wore braces on his legs from fifteen to eighteen months to help him learn to stand and begin to walk.

When Kory was two years old, I received a phone call that he had been rushed to the hospital because he had a seizure. The daycare director explained that he suddenly began to jerk during his playtime. Immediately, I left work with no hesitation. Once I arrived at the hospital, the doctors informed me that his seizure resulted from an extremely high fever that unexpectedly spiked out of nowhere. The next few months passed quickly. Finally, the time came to enroll him in an early childhood development program at three years old. The years continued to fly by swiftly.

At five years old, Kory began struggling in elementary school. I constantly received calls from his teachers, paras, and other staff informing me he would not do his work. Instead, he would stand up, walk around, and throw things around the classroom. He would even pick up the teacher's desk. I began receiving all sorts of complaints which led me to visit his school one day. I requested a consultation. During our meeting, I asked, *"Have you ever thought about the fact that maybe Kory does not understand you?"* I also stated, *"I do not think my son understands the rules here because, at home, he does not exhibit these behaviors. There is no abuse in our home. I do not scream or yell at my children. Kory is a very quiet kid. He never throws things or screams at home, so I believe something more is going on in his mind when he is here."*

Now, you must understand I had already been dismissed from two jobs by this time due to attendance issues. I had to leave work to go to Kory's schools sporadically because they constantly reported these bizarre behaviors to me. I specifically remember receiving the call that the school was planning to label him as a kid with behavioral problems. Well, I started doing some research and discovered dreadful information. Once a child is labeled with behavioral issues, it follows them for the remainder of their life. I refused to allow that to happen to my son, not my Kory.

I began to notice that when loud music came on, he would turn and tilt his head. His reaction to loud music was the same in the house, at church, or in the car. Each time, he would tilt his head up toward the right and give a side-eye look. Then one day, I noticed his forehead was starting to grow just a little. So, I made the first of many phone calls to Scottish Rite For Children. I called relentlessly for days hoping to secure an appointment for Kory.

I remember finally getting a nurse on the phone. Once I explained his symptoms to her, she hastily rushed the usually grueling call process. She rapidly transferred the call to the neurology department. The coordinator scheduled Kory for an appointment the same day with the neurologist. I took him to the facility. He had an EEG. Kory's new doctor said two words to us, *"Smoking Gun!"* The neurologist advised me that my son was having 26 to 40 staring seizures a day. His seizures were only lasting for a few deciseconds. Every time Kory had a seizure, his brain would stop functioning which meant that he would not remember what happened within those moments. I immediately started crying, but I abruptly stopped. I politely asked the doctor if Kory could have an MRI. The neurologist replied, *"No, he does not need one. We have already caught the seizures."* This time I stated, *"I am not asking you: I am telling you I want him to have an MRI."*

After a few more months went by, it was finally time for his MRI. When the results came back, the neurologist informed me Kory had a brain cyst. At this moment, the downward spiral began. I will be frank. Instead of praying, I started blaming myself. I blamed myself for all the choices I made regarding not having two parents in our household. I started thinking that maybe because I had a heart condition and had taken heart pills, I caused him to have all these problems. I started thinking perhaps he had this cyst because I cried all the time. I just kept blaming myself. Then depression tried to sneak in. An entire year went by, and it was time to have another MRI because we started monitoring the cyst. Another year passed right at the third-year mark. I will never forget those words, *"It is growing. It is no longer a cyst. It is now a brain tumor!"* All I could think about was my baby, who was now a young boy, going to multiple doctors, being stuck with needles week after week, month after month, and now year after year. Also, right before the tumor was discovered, they diagnosed him with Autism. In addition to those two diagnoses, he was diagnosed with a chromosome blood disorder.

Around this time, I was let go from another job and then another job. I am going to be completely honest here. As Kory's mother, his biggest fan, and his loudest cheerleader, I still was not 100% accepting his Autism diagnosis. I just kept telling myself, *"He is just a slow learner: everything is going to be okay."* It is not that I was ashamed. However, I just could *not* and would *not* accept it - if only you knew how many times I have cried. I will be even more candid. I still weep weekly in the wee hours of the night because I know that I cannot fix this. As a mother, you want to protect your children and help them in every way possible. Just imagine watching your child have seizures, getting stuck time after time, and you cannot help him. Within the last two years, Kory has been diagnosed with first-stage Lupus. I have continued to watch him mature through different phases of Autism as he grows older. He is becoming a very strong young man. I am incredibly proud of him.

There are so many things that I have learned from my sons. However, the three most important things that make me a better mother to my sons are my patience, understanding, and unconditional love.

*"God is our refuge and strength, A very present help in trouble."*
***Psalm 46:1 NKJV***

**Lella "Lelia" D. Henderson** was born in Monroe, Louisiana. Initially, she attended Pine Bluff University where she majored in Music. Eventually, she transferred to Grambling State University and majored in Business Management. Lelia is the mother of two sons, Karl Pollard, Jr. aka P.J. and Kory Pollard. She and her sons are currently residing in the Dallas- Fort Worth, Texas area. Lelia works for the Dallas-Fort Worth Independent School District. She is a singer and writer. Lelia attended the American Idol tryouts in 2005. She is currently a member of God's Purpose Band and Hard Drive Band. Lelia owns a Hat and Accessories boutique, Lakorle'. The store's name is a combination of both of her sons' names and hers.

She is a member of many Autism parenting groups.

**Connect with Lelia**

Email: lellahenderson18@gmail.com
Facebook: Henderson Songtrist Lelia
Instagram: JumpN2Success
YouTube: Sunny Sunshine The Singer

# *"Just Breathe"*

***by***

***Valerie Ann Freeman***

For the parents who have a child with Special Needs,
I want you to know that God is with you all,
And He will continue to supply your needs,
So **just breathe**.

God knows you are strong and the struggles are real,
I can identify and I know how you feel,
But **just breathe**.

Your child may be Special but it does not mean they are weird,
And if people give you an unkind look or act as if they are in fear,
Don't worry because God is always near,
So **just breathe**.

You may pray every day,
And often wonder why do I have a child with Special Needs,
And yes, at times, you might even cry,
It is ok, so go ahead and,
**Just breathe**.

You may ask yourself is it wrong for the way that I feel,
Not at all because you are human,
And the struggle is very real,
So **just breathe**.

Be encouraged and know for sure,
Your child feels your love,
Your baby is a gift from God,
So, give your child all your kisses and love,
so, you can **just breathe**!

***"Be strong and of good courage; do not be afraid, nor be dismayed, for the Lord your God is with you wherever you go."*** ***Joshua 1:9 NKJV***

# *"A New Normal: Life Forever Changed"*

*by*

***Kristina S. Toole***

Have you ever had your life change in an instant? You have this vision of what your life will be like, and then suddenly, a few words spoken by a physician brings that whole vision tumbling down. This scary, new normal is unlike any you can ever imagine, yet all you can do is cruise along for the ride.

Right before my thirty-third birthday in 2013, I found out I was pregnant with my second child. My husband Joseph and I had been married almost two years. We already had four children between the two of us. We were so excited to add this baby who would complete our perfectly blended family. Once we found out we were having a girl, we quickly chose Lakelyn Ann Toole's name. I would often wonder how she would look. Which one of her siblings would she look like, or would she resemble all of them in some way? Would she be her Daddy's hunting buddy? Would she love to dance like Payton? Would she watch SpongeBob with Ethan? There were so many questions. I could not wait to meet her!

Lakelyn made her quick, very hasty appearance on September 14, 2013 at 5:25 a.m. She was five weeks early and weighed 5 pounds 5 ounces. She was in the hospital nursery for almost nine days due to not gaining and maintaining enough weight, but she was never admitted to the NICU {Newborn Intensive Care Unit}. We were finally able to bring our perfect baby girl home. All was well the first three months. Lakelyn was growing and healthy. Then in November, at her two-month-old checkup, her pediatrician noticed she favored the right side of her head. She told me to put a towel or pillow under her head. Doing this would help her head to round out. Besides this, we had no indication of all that was to come.

The weekend before her first Christmas, Lakelyn began throwing up. I had returned to my job as a Human Resources Assistant. My mom was babysitting her for us during the day. My mom had become ill with a stomach virus, so we thought Lakelyn had it as well. She had thrown up that Friday night. Since she was still sick during the day on Saturday, I took her to the walk-in clinic that night. Due to her being so young, they recommended I take her to the hospital for further evaluation, so I did. Once I made it to the hospital, they hooked her up to an IV and ran lab work. It was late at night while we were there, and Lakelyn slept most of the time. The doctors did not have the opportunity to see her awake. Eventually, we were told she was not dehydrated. All of her other lab results were normal, so they discharged her. On Sunday, she became sick again. Joseph and I decided to take her to the pediatrician first thing in the morning.

It was a cold and dreary day. Monday, December 23, 2013 was the day our lives forever changed. We walked into the pediatrician's office thinking our sweet, beautiful, three- month-old daughter had a stomach virus. Only to be told by the nurse practitioner that there was something wrong with her brain. She told us her soft spot was bulging, and we needed to get to the hospital as soon as possible. A team would be waiting for us to perform an MRI and a CAT scan to figure out exactly what was wrong with Lakelyn. It was a whirlwind of doctors, nurses, and PICU {Pediatric Intensive Care Unit} staff that were running numerous tests on her from there.

The pediatric neurosurgeon told us that our baby had a massive brain tumor consuming the whole right side of her brain. It had most likely begun to grow and form like a normal cell in utero, which is why it was never detected. The neurosurgeon also informed us that she would need surgery to remove it and may have to go to St. Jude's for further treatment. These were crushing words that no parent should ever have to hear about their newborn, who had barely begun life. It felt like the room was spinning and this was a horrible nightmare we needed to wake up from, but could not. How could this be happening to our little Lakelyn? I could not even consider the possibility of her not making it. Could this have been detected sooner? What did I miss? What could I have done differently? So many questions and so many emotions were flowing through us! Never have I had a season in my life bring me to my knees such as this. All we could do was pray.

We almost lost Lakelyn on Christmas night. All of her vitals started to drop. Her blood pressure, pulse rate, and respiration rate plummeted. I remember her arm dropping with a thud listlessly when we grabbed it. Hearing all the monitors going off and beeping, then having nurses quickly usher us out of the PICU room was terrifying. It was the night before her craniotomy surgery to remove the brain tumor. The staff paged the neurosurgeon. He raced to the hospital within ten minutes. He successfully removed the fluid that was rapidly building up in her brain. By the time we were allowed back in her room, Lakelyn was fine and resting comfortably. We were able to breathe a sigh of relief that our sweet girl was all right. On December 26, 2013, Lakelyn underwent a craniotomy. The surgeon removed 100% of her tumor! Unfortunately, the doctors later determined that Lakelyn had a stroke right after the surgery. As a result, the left side of her body was weaker than the right side. She also stopped taking a bottle. A week after the first surgery, she had another surgery to place a feeding tube called a gastrostomy tube {G- tube}. The neurosurgeon also felt like she was exhibiting seizure-like activity, so he prescribed her first anti-seizure medication. All in all, Lakelyn was in the hospital for over a month.

As we exited the hospital with our now 4-month-old daughter, who had undergone the unimaginable, we entered into our new normal. We were beginning a whole new life filled with doctor's appointments, hospital stays, medical supplies, various medications, therapy appointments, routine lab work, MRIs, CAT scans, EEGs, and so many more unknowns.

We had no idea how much our lives had changed and would continue to change. Lakelyn had become sensory sensitive. Any loud noises would cause her to get upset. We had to keep the television volume down and speak quietly around her. Mickey Mouse Clubhouse® became her means of escape. We quickly realized she *loved* the "Hot Dog Dance" song. I cannot tell you how many times we would have to leave it on repeat for her. As the months went on, Lakelyn's pediatrician added more specialists to her care in New Orleans, Louisiana. These new facilities were four and a half hours from our home in Monroe, Louisiana. It seemed like something was going on every day. I had to stay on top of her schedule. Whether it was keeping her feeding schedule, hooking up the pump on time, making sure she had all her therapy, or scheduling doctor appointments for each week, I quickly realized that I would not be able to return to work because her care had to come first. Not just anyone could babysit Lakelyn for me now, and I certainly could not have her in daycare as sensitive and medically fragile as she was.

As painful as reliving Lakelyn's story can be, it is also incredibly beautiful. I realize Lakelyn's journey has opened our eyes to an awe-inspiring side of life where every small step is celebrated like a huge milestone. Although this was not *my* plan, this was most certainly God's plan for Lakelyn's life. She has touched countless lives through her testimonies shared on her Facebook page *"Lakelyn's Love."* Strangers from all over the United States and even other countries reach out to me because her triumphs touch them. They also pray with us for her when she is sick. It amazes me to think that *my* little girl has that effect on people. She is a remarkable example of how God can use our experiences for His purpose. No matter what you face in life, always keep God first and know that your beautiful story is waiting to be written.

***"You can make many plans, but the Lord's purpose will prevail."***
***Proverbs 19:21 NLT***

**Kristina Somoza Toole** is the oldest of two daughters born to Marty and Carlos Somoza, along with her sister, Katie. Other than three years living in Memphis, Tennessee, Kristina was raised in Monroe, Louisiana. She is most thankful that her parents instilled in her that God comes first in all you do. Even when she did not deserve His grace, love, and mercy, our Heavenly Father never gave up on her. Kristina is a graduate of the University of Louisiana at Monroe. She graduated with a Bachelor of General Studies degree. Although she never really knew what she wanted to do in life, she truly enjoyed working in Human Resources until her daughter Lakelyn got sick. Since then, she has been a very busy stay-at-home mom.

Kristina and her husband, Joseph, have been married for ten years. God has blessed her with two daughters, Payton and Lakelyn. In addition, she has three bonus children: Selina, Ethan, and Baleigh. Joseph and Kristina have three grandsons and a fourth grandson on the way. Kristina enjoys reading, traveling when possible, and spending time with friends and family. God has truly blessed her.

**Connect with Kristina**
Email: k_somoza@yahoo.com
Facebook: Kristina Somoza Toole
Instagram: Kristina S. Toole

# *"Matters Of The Heart"*

***by***

***Tramelria D. James***

*Mrs. James, I need to know: when you leave this office, will you go straight to the hospital, or should I call an ambulance to take you guys?"* With that one mind-jarring question, my journey into motherhood navigated down a path I had never imagined.

My initial introduction to *The G.U.D. Life* began in 1988. My youngest sister, Whitney, was born with Downs Syndrome. She was our family's sunshine on a rainy day. Her personality and character radiated everywhere she went! Unfortunately, during the late 1980s, there were not many resources available in our community. So, my mother did the necessary research to locate different organizations that would help with Whitney's developmental wellness. My mother felt so blessed to find an organization called 'Families Helping Families.' It was terrific watching Whitney excel with the newfound therapies and techniques our family learned to help her. My mother then began to share this information with other families affected by Down Syndrome and Special Needs. I recall watching my mother interacting and bonding with my sister. The look of adoration covering her face when they connected melted my heart. The immense patience displayed when hurdles were thrown at her regarding Whitney's well-being was a strength like no other. In reality, observing her set the tone for how I would govern my role as Whitney's sibling, an aunt to my nephew, a confidante to my best friend, and prepared me for my journey with my only son.

In early October 2005, our sweet baby boy was born. He was an absolute joy. We were smitten with his adorableness. Being a new mom, I was very attentive to his needs. I made sure that he was present for every appointment and that his vaccines were administered according to schedule. I closely monitored his height, weight, and all other necessary things. Memorial Day Weekend 2007, I was preparing to go to work. As I was putting my shoes on, God spoke to me just as clear as day. He said, *"Call in."* I began to question this decision since I hardly ever called in ~ especially when nothing was wrong.

Nevertheless, I obediently called into work. A few minutes later, C.J. woke up. Instantly, I could see that he did not feel well. I quickly made an appointment with his pediatrician. They proceeded to do a routine check-up. However, they omitted the step of reading his oxygen level. The nurse corrected her misstep and checked it. As she retrieved and reviewed the result, I noticed the concerned expression on her face. I fervently started praying for God's hedge of protection over my child.

Shortly after, the doctor entered and revealed that C.J.'s oxygen level was 84 {which is low}. His x-rays showed swelling around his heart. My own heart dropped into the pit of my stomach while fresh tears stung my eyes. She then directed me to go to the hospital expeditiously. I wondered how my son could have serious health issues at the tender age of eighteen months? I challenged myself, trying to recall any signs that I might have missed. Finally, I called my husband and my mom to inform them of this emergent crisis. They both immediately agreed to meet me there. I loaded him into the vehicle, said a prayer asking God to give me strength, and rushed him to the hospital. Upon arriving, they performed some confirmation tests and shipped us via ambulance to the next major city. An ambulance ride was a significant feat due to him already not feeling well. We had to separate during the ride, as I could not ride in the back with him. There was a whirlwind of emotions vexing my mind. I had never even ridden in an ambulance myself at twenty-five years old, and here my son was taking one very early in his life. After a slightly less than two-hour ride, we made it safely. My husband drove our vehicle behind us, and we desperately marched into the hospital to get some answers to the critical situation unfolding right before our eyes.

Once we made it to the hospital, more extensive testing began. The test results revealed that C.J. had a condition known as Atrioventricular Canal Defect. In layman's terms, there was a hole that reached all four chambers of my baby's heart. This defect resulted in a major leak within the valves that regulated his blood flow. As a result, the doctors informed us that our precious baby boy would undergo open- heart surgery. Devastation crept into my mind. Anguish captured my heart. I probed my brain trying to remember what I possibly had done wrong. Would our baby survive this surgery? If he did, what quality of life would he have?

Now, as I reflect, I think of the teachings of my Pastor and First Lady. They have taught us that weapons may form against us, but they will not prosper. {Isaiah 54:17} Although Jesus endured many trials during His time on Earth, I am reminded that I am certainly no better than him! He suffered hardships, so shall we! I had to identify the good in this capacity. Only 54% of infants survive without medical intervention, 35% until twelve months, and 15% until twenty- four months. Here our son was eighteen months old! We had no clue whatsoever, he had no symptoms, and we had no idea at all! Even though we were going through tribulations, God was still keeping us! To God be the Glory!

C.J.'s operation was scheduled for November 13, 2007. I made it my number one priority to educate myself as much as possible about his condition. Our friends and family rallied around us with love and support. We had to travel to a Children's Specialty Hospital which was five hours away from our home. Not knowing how long recovery would be after the surgery, we utilized the Ronald McDonald House of South Louisiana. They specialize in supporting traveling families by providing a room, boarding, and meals. The staff was terrific. They truly cared. There were so many other families staying there. It was indeed a blessing not having to worry about those necessities as we faced what was to come. The night before his surgery, I was extremely restless. I cried out to God and asked for His incomparable grace and mercy. I began to speak over my son's life courageously and recalled some of God's promises! {2 Corinthians 12:9 and Isaiah 46:4}. The following day, we woke up early and went to the hospital to be admitted for the surgery. Although I prayed, I was a ball of nerves. The staff came to take him back. We fiercely loved on him.

The duration was two hours. Following many tears and prayers, the physicians informed us that the surgery was a success! Afterward, seeing him connected to various machines and being in a medically induced coma severely tugged at my heart, but I persevered to ensure that his recovery went as smoothly as possible. We stayed two and a half weeks in the hospital. We faced several obstacles. We were not allowed to hold him due to his chest tubes. His diet was restricted to fluids only and not too many because of the drainage. It was difficult not to care for him as I usually did, but we gradually adapted. Soon after, we were discharged and returned home to start our new routine.

Since then, he has flourished and grown. He will be sixteen years old this year. He is a well-rounded, respectful, handsome, and God-fearing young man. Participating in sports, making friends, playing video games, going to church, and loving family is what he loves to do now. Subsequently, he has not had any complications, although his condition is a lifelong plight.

Eventually, we all will face adversities on this quest we know as life. I truly believe that God has been equipping me since I was eight years old for this assignment. He allowed me to obtain the knowledge and skills that I would need to show compassion in my biological family, my community, and my twenty-year career as a medical professional. Be encouraged and stand firm in your faith. Challenging moments might arise, but know that you are resilient! Always remember that you are chosen to love one of *God's Unique Designs* and there is an incredible community behind you filled with love, support, and encouragement!

> ***"When my heart is overwhelmed; Lead me to the rock that is higher than I."*** ***Psalm 61:2 NKJV***

**Tramelria D. Johnson-James** was born and raised in Monroe, Louisiana. She is the second born of seven siblings. Her family and friends have always described her as very caring. She has always believed that God blessed her with a nurturing essence. Her valuable gift has remained an essential quality that perfectly aligns with her professional career. She has been happily enjoying her career in the medical field for over twenty years.

Her faith, family, and friends are among the most important things in her life. She loves the Lord with all of her heart. However, her roles as wife and mother are the parts of her life that make her whole.

She is committed to bringing awareness to the Special Needs Community with her principal focus on Down Syndrome, Heart Defects, and Autism. In addition, Tramelria is an avid reader, which has guided her to broaden her horizon by becoming an Author.

Tramelria resides in Monroe with her husband, son, daughter, and the family's pet dog.

**Connect with Tramelria**

Email: tramelrajames@gmail.com

# *"Finding Your Why"*

***by***

***Tameka C. Burns***

Life is mysterious. We may plan to do certain things or have an idea of a particular career we want to pursue. However, God has a way of putting us in the places where we are meant to be. He will cause us to become uneasy until we do what we are called and chosen to do. It may take time to figure out what we should be doing, but He *will* guide us to it. It took ten years in administrative roles and a college degree in Business, but I finally figured out what I was purposed to be doing and *why* I was chosen for the task. This is my story.

I started working at the age of fifteen. By the time I was twenty, I just felt like I wanted to be in an administrative role. The last position I held before realizing my calling required me to get my bachelor's degree to receive a better job title with better pay. I did just that. Unfortunately, I was informed that they did not have the funding for my new role in the budget the day before my graduation. Therefore, after working full- time and going to school full-time simultaneously, I ended up in the same position that my supervisor initially hired me to fill. I was upset and felt like giving up, but I stayed the course even after receiving the disappointing news. At that time, I did not realize God made me uncomfortable in order to move me to something greater. Despite the treatment from my peers, which clearly revealed my harsh reality, I continued to run from what I should be doing because I genuinely believed I had a good job.

A part of my life that has nothing to do with my previous career choices is my love for working with children. I cannot have children of my own, so I poured into others like they were mine. Over the years, I have tutored children since I was about twelve years old. I continued tutoring children even during the years leading up to this. I love to watch them find their strength and see them become empowered. It gives me so much joy to see their faces when they accomplish something they once believed they could not do. Yet, even with all of the indicators, the thought of becoming a teacher still never crossed my mind.

In May of 2011, I was sitting at my desk researching a grant. While I was sitting there, I began typing my resignation letter. I decided to go back to school to become a teacher. There was no hesitation in my thought process. I did not feel nervous about my actions at all. It was a done deal. I walked out of my office that day and enrolled in school to work on my Master's in Special Education.

I have always had a desire to help children with Special Needs. Some people who are close to me made me want to do more to help. I would listen and observe the emotional responses from situations taking place with them at school. I desired to be a voice for them to ensure they were all treated like the "normal" kids. I know from experience that kids who tend to be a little "different" are often teased and even overlooked. I was a gifted student. Other students frequently teased us because we were in a separate area of the school. I finally accepted the fact that this was my calling! Previously, God had given me all of these "good" jobs. Now He had given me a career because this is my *why*. I used to wonder, *"Why am I here?"* I now know it is because God chose me to serve these babies who do not have a voice or cannot voice their feelings.

I started teaching in 2011. Over the past ten years, I realized that I was placed in the classroom for them and myself. My students have taught me some valuable lessons and made me appreciate life more. I have gone to my car several days and cried because hearing my students' circumstances broke me down. After I dried my tears, I would return to the building ready to keep fighting for my babies. I would fight to correct every issue I could just for my students. I go into the classroom with a mission to make each day count when I step foot in the school.

The thought of never having children of my own truly bothered me at one point. But now, every student that has come into my class has left as my baby. These connections help settle the mental torment of never being a mother. God's plan is evident once you step back and let Him work.

I realized early in my teaching career that the students needed an advocate, as well as some of their parents. Therefore, I go above and beyond to ensure that my parents know their rights. Once we connect, the parents and I work together to do what is best for their child from that point on. I was shocked when I realized so many parents did not know all of the rights in place for their children. At that moment, I knew God chose me to take on this role to advocate for them. Becoming a Special Education teacher is indeed my calling. God led me to this because I can help make life so much easier for my students and their parents.

I have dealt with some harsh realities while being an advocate, teacher, and school parent to my students. There were days where I sat and wondered about students after they left for the day. What are their home lives like? Do they eat before going to bed? Did they bathe before bed? Do they even have a bed? These are actual day-to-day problems for some of my babies. It has led me to become more proactive by talking to them on an even closer personal level. I allow my students to become so comfortable with me that they will tell me just about anything. Honestly, I do not want to know some things! Whew! Be that as it may, I listen because I would rather them tell me instead of holding it all in. I carry their problems with me hoping to make it easier for them.

On that note, I want to say that many people have misconceptions about children with Special Needs. They think these innocent babies really do not have feelings and do not actually think about themselves differently. The people who think this way are sadly mistaken. They can feel if a person likes them or not. They can tell when an individual does not want to be bothered with them. They know they are different from the rest of the children. They spend so much time trying to fit in with the rest when all along they were born to stand out. Let them stand out! They are unique and wonderfully made. I constantly tell my babies they are different because God took extra time shining and polishing them into beautiful diamonds.

If you are a parent to a child with Special Needs, please talk to them about it. I have experienced a student on the verge of committing suicide at the age of twelve because he was "different" and did not know or understand why. His family never took the time to explain to him what he was facing. I called him to my room and explained to him that he had Autism! We watched some videos which showed other Autistic children. He pointed out a boy in the video and told me he acts like him. I told him, *"See, you are not that different after all." There are others just like you. You are different from some of your peers, but there is nothing wrong with that at all. Stand out and shine!"*

In closing, just like I told my student to stand out and shine, we all have the potential to do just that. Whatever you do day-to-day, put your best foot forward and do it with validity. You were placed here to do something special. God chose you to be your best self in some capacity.

So, seek it out and trust God to guide you through your process because knowing your *why* can be so rewarding! God is love!

***"The righteous cry out, and the LORD hears, and delivers them out of all their troubles."***
***Psalm 34:17 KJV***

**Tameka Calhoun-Burns** was born in Shreveport, Louisiana. She currently resides in Monroe, Louisiana. She has been married to Robert for fourteen years and has a twenty-two- year-old stepson, Robert Jr. Eight years ago, she became a dog- mom to her Pitbull, Duchess. She is a member of Union Missionary Baptist Church in Bosco, Louisiana.

She was raised by her grandparents because her mother had her at the age of fifteen. At twenty, her mother was diagnosed with Lupus. The doctors gave her only two years to live. However, God gave her twenty-six more years. Tameka unexpectedly lost her mother on December 26, 2009 which was exactly one week after Tameka received her Bachelor's Degree. The loss changed her life drastically.

People have always told Tameka that she is wise for her age. She believes it is due to her grandparents' upbringing. She is supremely empathic and goes above and beyond to help others. She received both her Bachelor's and Master's degrees from the University of Louisiana at Monroe in Monroe, Louisiana. She is a Special Education teacher in the public school system. She chose a career in Special Education to be a voice for the voiceless and make people more aware of children with Special Needs.

In her free time, she loves decorating, completing D-I-Y projects, spending time fishing, cooking, and taking care of her family.

**Connect with Tameka**

Email: mizzmeka_98@hotmail.com

# *"Special Needs"*

***by***

***Valerie Ann Freeman***

**S** is for I have **Special** Needs,

**P** is for **Perfect** which I am in God's eyes,

**E** is for **Excel** and win in everything that I do,

C is for **Cry** which I sometimes do,

**I** is for yes, I am very **Intelligent** and very much creative,

**A** is for I am an **Angel** in my parent's eyes,

**L** is for when I **Laugh** because I am so elated.

**N** is for **Never** is there a dull moment with me,

**E** is because I am **Eager** to have a good time,

**E** is so you will let the negative thoughts you have of me **Exit**

from your mind,

**D** is so now we can **Dance,** smile, and drink a diet coke,

**S** is sometimes I am very **Serious**, but just like you, I often like to crack a joke,

because **SPECIAL NEEDS** individuals have fun too!

***"Before I made you in your mother's womb, I knew you. Before you were born, I chose you for a special work." Jeremiah 1:4-5 ERV***

# *"I Love You, Grammy!"*

***by***
***Jacqueline D. Sims***

Love is a many splendored thing! Love is beautiful! One of the most adorable loving relationships is the one between a grandmother and her grandchild. The bond between a grandmother and her grandchild is priceless. I have many precious examples of a grandmother's love. My grandmothers, aunts, family members, family friends, and loved ones were all grandmothers to be emulated. The example of a grandmother's care that I observed the most was between my dear mother and her grandchildren. I was blessed to have the most loving model of giving and receiving a grandmother's love and care. My mother truly loved being a grandmother. Her face just glowed whenever she was around her grandchildren. My daughter would climb onto my mother's lap and give her the biggest hugs. My son would stand on the couch and plant the sweetest and wettest kisses on her cheek. My nieces and nephews would shower her with love and affection. They would all tell her, *"I love you, Grammy!"* The emotional floods of joy and happiness that were on her face were priceless and beyond comparison. I would sit and watch for hours thinking, *"I cannot wait to feel that loving feeling and to hear those sweet words."*

Of course, there was never any doubt about what my grandchildren would call me 'Grammy'! My mother passed away in October of 1995; therefore, she did not experience seeing me as a grandmother. Nevertheless, she left such a rich and inspiring legacy of love and compassion. It was happening! My dream was coming true! I was going to be a Grandmother!

On April 9, 2000, Jayla was born! I felt a new love and deeper level of joy flooding my heart that I had never felt in my life. *I was finally a Grammy!* While standing at the window of the nursery watching my sweet, precious angel, I never would have imagined the health challenges Jayla would face in the near future. Jayla grew and was a playful and chipper baby. She was a happy and loving baby. Then, she took her 18-month immunizations. Immediately, we noticed a change in her personality and temperament. She became withdrawn and detached. She rejected social interaction with us.

She refused to accept any gestures of love or affection from us. We took her to her pediatrician. We explained something had changed, and Jayla was different. Her physician began running a battery of tests. Diagnosis: Autism!

*"What did you say, doctor?"* We had heard of Autism, but had never been affected by it. What were these new terms? Autism Spectrum Disorder? High-functioning? Cognitive Impairment? Autism affects how a person perceives the outside world and

interacts with others. This condition can cause issues with social interactions, communication skills, learning, and the ability to function independently. Autism can also cause a person to respond to typical everyday situations inappropriately.

When an illness, disease, or condition has never touched a person, that individual never really needed to actually understand it! The inability to communicate is one of the symptoms of Autism. Think about the feeling of trying to find the appropriate words to console someone who is grieving. It is a real struggle! The task of trying to communicate is a daily struggle for people with Autism. The hardest thing I ever heard was that my only grandchild might not be able to show different emotions.

What about *love*? Would I ever hear my granddaughter tell me she loves me? The thought of not hearing her say, *"I love you, Grammy!"* was nearly unbearable. I am a Christian who believes in Jesus Christ! I believe He was crucified on the cross for my sins. He rose with *all power* in His hands, and His healing power for all manner of diseases! God had shown us His ability by healing Jayla many times. He brought her through numerous brain surgeries. We began to ask for our faithful God's healing touch again!

There are times that He does miraculous {instantaneous} healings! Other times He heals through medication. Finally, sometimes healing comes through a process! For example, we have watched God healing her through a gradual process. Jayla was very withdrawn when she was initially diagnosed. She wanted little contact or cuddling from us, but God has steadily healed her!

We continued to shower her with love even though she did not know how to accept it. We never stopped praying and believing. St. Mark 11:24 says, *"Therefore I say unto you, "What things soever ye desire, when ye pray, believe that ye receive them, and ye shall have them."* I had a personal prayer request: *"God, please let me hear my first grandchild tell me, "I love you, Grammy!" in Jesus' name, Amen."* I never stopped believing, waiting, or expecting.

The first time I heard Jayla tell me that she loved me, I screamed! Tears immediately flowed from my eyes! When she initiated hugging me, I thought, *"Our God does hear and answer prayer!"* One of my favorite scriptures came to mind St. Mark 9:23, *"Jesus said unto him, "If thou canst believe, all things are possible to him that believeth."*

Jayla has the most beautiful contagious laugh now! She has a smile that lights up an entire room! She is playful and happy! She is initiating new ways to communicate! Jayla and I text and Facetime daily. I consistently receive the incredible blessing of hearing her tell me, *"I love you, Grammy!"* Jayla is our *miracle* and she is truly a *blessing* to everyone she meets!

Live with *expectation* daily!
Keep *hope* alive!
*Never* give up!
Do not ever stop *believing*!
Celebrate *all* victories!

***"And he said, "The things which are impossible with men are possible with God."*** ***St. Luke 18:27 KJV***

**Jacqueline Denise Sims** is a Christian gifted in the areas of helps, hospitality, and giving. She has served as a Sunday School teacher, Bible study teacher, choir member, greeter, hospitality aide, usher board member, and pastor's aide member. Jacqueline is inspired by her love of helping people learn God's Holy Word. She has written several biblical books. For approximately five years, Jacqueline wrote and published four books per year ~ one each quarter. She authored Sunday School Lesson companion game books which contained crossword puzzles, fill-in-the-blank, word searches, and other games.

As a child, Jacqueline was always concerned about the feelings of others. Her nature was noticeably sympathetic and empathetic. As a woman of God, she consistently supports people through difficult and trying times. She has a "smile" ministry that aims to bring smiles to people's faces anywhere and everywhere she goes. She enthusiastically loves to empower and uplift others. Jacqueline is passionate about helping people live with more hope, expectation, joy, peace, and happiness. To evolve with modern technology, Jacqueline now has a flourishing text messaging ministry. She sends hundreds of motivational messages daily, which include scriptures. In addition, she spreads The Gospel through her social media and greeting card ministries. Her heart desires to live in the will of God. She loves God, His people, and teaching The Holy Word.

Jacqueline loves her family. She has been happily married to her high school sweetheart, George I, for 45 years. She is a proud mother, grandmother, godmother, and mother-in-love. She is the oldest of five siblings. She was born and raised in Monroe, Louisiana. She has lived in Louisiana, Alabama, Mississippi, and now resides in Texas.

**Connect with Jacqueline**
Email: jcqsms715@outlook.com

# *"When An Answer Is Not The Answer"*

*by*

***Shana C. Hubbard***

Relating to our children and our lives, we must understand that we are in this world, but not of this world. {John 17:14 NKJV} Therefore, maintaining a healthy balance between the natural and spiritual of what is, what should be, and what is to come is essential to cultivating a balanced and well-rounded life for us as individuals, parents, and valuable representations of Christians within our society, families, and communities.

As a Christian parent, while carrying my son, I sought and heard from God about the call on his life and why he was being brought into the world. He clearly revealed it to me, so I knew who and what my son was destined to be. However, I did not know the things that I would have to endure to get him there. Neither did I know the things he would have to face on the road to his life's destiny. As we travel life's journey, it is essential to search and seek those things required to transition us to the places we will end up in life. During our search and seek, we will receive answers. They are just not always what we want to hear or what we believe they should be.

Parents are the first to recognize the majority of the things that happen with their children, especially related to their growth, milestones, and development. We are the first to know when something seems wrong, off, or abnormal. Considering this, we must also be mindful not to overlook or miss critical indicators that have become normal to us, our household, and what is deemed normal to our family's generational makeup. We must appreciate, respect, and observe what the medical professionals share with us as a gauge, such as growth charts. Those tools assist us in ensuring that our children reach milestones and the necessary targets for their age groups.

And this is where my testimony begins.

My son was born five weeks early due to low amniotic fluid, which caused him to be at risk of cord strangulation. His medical team decided it was best to deliver him immediately. Thankfully, though early, he did not require a NICU visit.

Everything else surrounding his birth plan and process was normal. As he grew, though premature, he quickly advanced on the full-term baby growth chart in every area, hitting all targeted milestones. However, we noticed that he was behind in his speech and the number of words he should have been speaking at almost a year old. He was making sounds, responsive, and all the usual things, but not using many "words." I continued to monitor his progress and mentioned it in one of his regular pediatric visits. I explained how he was finding what seemed to be a different way to communicate other than talking. He would grab us to get what he wanted, shake his head, grunt, gibber, or cry. However, he would not clearly verbalize his expressions and was not always using actual words. The pediatrician advised us that this could be normal since he understood everything we said, or it could be him deciding not to talk yet. However, due to my pressing desire to ensure that all was well, he referred us to a neurologist.

The first neurological evaluation included a plethora of questions for us as parents. It required us to explain how my son expressed or communicated particular needs and desires. The neurologist diagnosed my son at almost two years old with early signs of ADHD. As a praying mother, my spirit and observation did not receive this diagnosis as *the answer*, but simply *an* answer. It was up to us to decide what to do with the information. My response to the diagnosis became prayers for direction. I rebuked anything and everything the enemy would try to speak over and into my son's life that was *not* divinely ordered by God, for him to go through or grow through, to get him to the place that I knew God had destined for him to be. We would endure God's plan, but we would not embrace anything sent by the enemy that God didn't have in his plan for us.

As a parent, I realized early on that it is my responsibility and position to fight, war, and pray over all the places and paths my son must take along the way. We were committed to positioning him to become and understand what God has called him to become. As parents, we must maintain this position until our children can understand and take their proper stance. Once our children come into the knowledge, our role in that place is to support them, simply from a different posture and perspective.

My son was now two years old. He began to speak more, but his speech was still unclear. We also discovered he was now able to read! Our son's reading surpassed his ability to talk. He was not just reading small three or four-letter words. He was reading big words. He read building signs while riding in the car and called out the names of other cars as we passed by. He was doing addition and subtraction with flashcards and blocks. We knew all these things were very advanced for his age group. He just could not always "say" things clearly.

My prayers and diligence for my son led me to a second neurologist. He was diverse, inclusive, and had more experience with varying ethnicities. This appointment was *terrific*! He advised us that the initial diagnosis of ADHD was a stereotype and not accurate or appropriate for my son's case. He explained that in his experience, ADHD is always one of the common diagnoses given to young boys when there seems to be an issue or something that is not entirely understood. He thoroughly evaluated our son. After a series of tests, he advised us, *"Mr. & Mrs. Hubbard, you guys are working with a genius boy! He does not have ADHD, Autism, or Asperger's. He does not have any of that! However, he does have a severe language delay. He needs speech therapy, speech therapy, speech therapy! The more speech therapy he receives, the more you will see all the other 'issues' diminish. He is trying to find any way to communicate and express himself. Simply because he is unable to do it the way he hears it. As he learns to speak and his vocabulary expands, all of those 'issues' will be replaced with words!"*

The new diagnosis we received registered within my spirit. It made perfect sense regarding everything we had been experiencing. Finally, we understood why he would cry or scream during circle time at daycare while they were trying to learn ABCs and 123s. Since he was nine months old, he has recited his ABCs, reading, and solving math problems. Therefore, at this point, he was bored. Unfortunately, he could not say it. He could only show it!

Even though we now had an answer, it was time to plan. This is where the need for balance came into play. As I stated previously, at the onset, we must know what God has said and declared concerning our children, and a healthy balance is imperative. Now there was an issue present, and as the parent, I had a responsibility to find the answer to what was next. It was essential to figure out the plan to move us to the expected end.

We were directed to our local school district for therapy due to our private insurance not covering speech therapy unless needed due to an injury. Unfortunately, this process was a disaster. When parents are not familiar or experienced with the school district's IEP's, certain methods, and specific procedures, their child can experience more negative results than positive working with professionals.

We went into the school district needing speech therapy. We thoroughly explained all about our son, his needs, his way of communication and emphasized his level of advancement academically. The staff assured us they would handle everything in the classroom appropriately for him. However, he was not being taught on his academic level as promised. He was placed in a classroom with students who required more direct care and attention. He began to mimic his classmates' behavior. As a result, he also needed a behavioral therapist. Imagine had we not been diligent, consistent, present at the school, and prayerful. We would not have gotten to the bottom of what was happening in the classroom and why our son was experiencing this drastic behavior change that was only happening at the school. We immediately removed him from the school and found other solutions. This decision led to finding his blessed place! He is still receiving speech therapy. However, he has avoided many challenges and is now an overcomer because we did not take every answer as *the answer*!

I want to leave parents with this message. No matter the answers you receive concerning your child, be diligent, consistent, prayerful, and balanced to ensure your child receives the care they need that aligns with God's plan for your child's life. An answer is not always *the answer*! The ultimate answer comes *only* from God! Know what God has spoken and declared about your child and stand on it. Seek Him daily for all the *final* answers concerning what to do and the directions to take. God is our source! All other things are resources, but every resource is not the GOD resource directly set for our life and situation!

Just like us, your story may still be in process. Therefore, as we walk out the paths leading our children to their successes, be encouraged, and seek the One who always has *the answer*!

> ***"In the day of my trouble I will call upon You, For You will answer me."***
> ***Psalm 86:7 NKJV***

**Shoshana "Shana" Coleman Hubbard** is a native of Huntsville, Alabama. She currently resides in the Dallas-Fort Worth Metroplex with her husband, Antonio, and her only son, Preston Thomas. Shana is an anointed woman of honor and character who exemplifies class, grace, and integrity at all times. She believes that operating in excellence is imperative, no matter the task.

Shana holds a Master of Business Administration and is currently completing her licensure to become a Licensed Marriage and Family Therapist. She is a licensed Evangelist, called to prayer and intercession. She is passionate about teaching, training, giving, mission work, and deliverance.

After having a colorful career in various corporate analytic and consulting roles, Mrs. Hubbard holds a senior-level role for a leading software and technology company. In addition, Shana founded PACS – Life Lab, a non-profit organization that assists individuals in reaching their goals through literacy, training, education, and LOVE! She also founded Prestigious Administrative and Consulting Services, an executive administrative and consulting firm.

The favor, call, gifts, and wisdom of God have always been evident in her life! She is a confidante to many. She also has a God-given mandate as a generational curse breaker to continue to Champion the Cause of Jesus Christ!

**Connect with Shana**
Email: shanachubbard@gmail.com
Facebook: Shana C. Hubbard
Instagram: shanachubbard
www.prestigiousacs.com
www.pacslifelab.com
#PrestonsChronicles

# *"I Am Able"*

***by***

***Valerie Ann Freeman***

I may have an Intellectual Disability,
Which is a delay or lack of skills,
but a low IQ does not mean that
I am not human or do not feel,
So, please know that
**I am able.**

I may have Autism,
Which might restrict my interests and activities,
Cause communication difficulties,
but I do not lack in my creativities,
So, know that
**I am able.**

Downs Syndrome is very visible because of some physical development characteristics,
But because my looks are different does not mean I am unintelligent, because
**I am able.**

I may not see very well or perhaps I may be Visually Impaired or I may even be Blind,
So, if you see me crossing the street,
please be my eyes because I surely do not mind,
but do not forget
**I am able.**

I may have Tumors - large or small,

They may grow fast, slow, or not at all,
Either way, I am still a child of the Highest God,
And I want everyone to know that
**I am able.**

My Heart may have a Defect,
Abnormal, irregular, or damaged,
But only because of the grace of God,
I live with it and can manage, because
**I am able.**

I may have a Behavior Disorder,
Which means I cannot always
control my actions, attitude, or manners,
and I may draw some unfavorable reactions, but still,
**I am able.**

So please don't judge me by
my Medical Condition or my Diagnosis,
Whether mental, physical, emotional, or otherwise,
Just know that I am loved by my parents and my family too,
and I am an apple in God's eyes because
**He makes me able.**

*"Keep me as the apple of Your eye."*
***Psalm 17:8 NIV***

**Valerie Ann Freeman** was born and raised in the City of Brotherly Love, Philadelphia, Pennsylvania. She currently resides in Texas by way of Los Angeles, California, with her husband, Daniel, and her mother. Her mother's name is Valerie as well. She is proud to be her namesake because it allows her to be Valerie, Jr.! The name Valerie means "strong." Strong is precisely what she is because the joy of the Lord is her strength.

God blessed her to begin writing poetry in 1979 when He saved her. He also gifted her to become a songwriter, a poet, as well as a published author. Her first CD entitled "Free at Last" based on St. John 8:36 is available on Spotify.

Her passion is showing love and concern by visiting Special Needs adults, children, and babies. She especially enjoys spending time with her older sister, who struggles with mental challenges but can successfully learn and understand many things with guidance. Her sister has been in her care for sixteen years and is the love of her life. Together, they have met many and still face some challenges, but God has brought them through each one of them as He promised in Deuteronomy 31:8.

Her other passion is helping the homeless, whom she affectionately calls her "babies." She is elated when she has the opportunity to feed them, make care packages, volunteer at food banks, or goes to the homeless shelters to assist in serving them food. It brings so much joy and happiness to her heart seeing their smiles and receiving their hugs. Valerie knows that having agape love and deep empathy for people is a gift from God Almighty that He has bestowed on her heart. She feels incredible knowing that extending love with open arms makes their day, but little do they know ~ they actually make her day.

My **Bio** Is Just My **B**eginning To **I**nspire **O**thers!

**Connect with Valerie**
Facebook: Valerie Freeman

# *"Green Light Grace"*

***by***

***Shervondaline S. Breedlove***

*"They are slicing my baby's head open!"*

"Oh my God, Shervon, do *not* say it *like* that!" my mom shrieked after I made that statement while waiting in the hallway for Jayla's hospital room to be assigned.

Our day started great! I printed the MapQuest directions to Jayla's new pediatrician whose Google reviews were fantastic. I was so excited about being in a new state and looking forward to countless new beginnings. Jayla was dressed beautifully in a bright shade of yellow from head-to-toe for her first doctor's visit in Mississippi. She received so many compliments as we were welcomed into the new office. Dr. Wilson was very soft-spoken, thorough, and knowledgeable. I felt so good about her examination. The doctor and nurse stepped out of the room after Jayla's check-up concluded. After a few minutes, the kind nurse returned to calmly inform me that I needed to take my precious new infant to the children's hospital directly across the street. In a matter of seconds, my cheerful and optimistic outlook, which perfectly matched Jayla's outfit, quickly shifted to startled and overwhelmed. As soon as we arrived, the hospital staff grabbed my beautiful baby and rushed away in the opposite direction. Then a massive set of metal doors slammed behind them. Immediate panic, anxiety, dizziness, numbness, shock, shakiness, and uncontrollable tears hit me all at once. The nurses brought a gurney into the hallway because it appeared that I was going to pass out.

About an hour later, a neurology care coordinator came into her hospital room. I was still in a daze. So, I saw her lips moving, but I was not hearing or registering any of the words she said. She proceeded to hand me a stack of books about Hydrocephalus, AV/VP shunts, necessary operation details, and recovery. I said, "Thank you." as I thought to myself, *"Ma'am, I could not read one word in these books - even if you paid me right now!"* At times, I still tremble when I think about the broad range of emotions that I felt in those one thousand four hundred forty minutes.

Jayla's brand new pediatrician cared enough to come and check on her that evening after clinic ended in her office. She explained that she knew Jayla needed the critical procedure because she observed her *"sunset eyes."* It is one of the most significant symptoms of Hydrocephalus, a condition caused by fluid buildup in the cavities deep within the brain. The excess fluid increases the size of the ventricles and puts pressure on the brain. As a result, Jayla had an emergency brain surgery to implant a VP Shunt. The shunt would relieve the pressure by draining the excess fluid from her brain into her abdomen, which her kidneys would then excrete.

She also assured us that Jayla was in the best hands with her new world-renowned neurosurgeon.

Although he was a spectacular brain specialist, he spoke very directly during our conversation. After the surgery, he said, *"We will have to wait and see how her body responds to the device. Since she is so young, she might not ever walk, talk, grow, or do anything."* I heard *every* word that he said, but I did *not* accept them. Instead, I began speaking The Word of God over her life that day. And I still do to this very day. This entire experience led me to start praying, fasting, and believing in a whole new way. I was seeking God because I wanted Him to heal my baby. Also, I needed Him to grant me an abundance of His peace, gentleness, hope, wisdom, and strength to be her mom.

Jayla's operation was a success. I carefully listened to the nurse's instructions, asked several questions, and tried to quickly adapt to the idea of cleaning and dressing her scars on my own. My family and friends have always teased me about being 'heavy-handed,' so learning to be gentle was a big deal for me. Gradually, I learned to comb her hair without being afraid of possibly dislodging her shunt. I purchased all educational toys, books, music, and videos for her. I was determined that she *would* do all the things that her neurosurgeon warned me that she *might* not do. Her recovery was uneventful. She was progressing normally. Jayla began walking at nine months old and talking right on target for her age. Our entire family, our friends, Dr. Wilson, and her neurosurgeon were thrilled and proud: Jayla was doing well. She was such a happy baby. However, a few days after her eighteen-month shots, we noticed drastic changes in her behavior and demeanor.

Most importantly, Jayla stopped talking, became very distant and unaffectionate. She even started to beat herself in the head and chest ferociously. My parents, brother, and I were baffled because she quickly transformed: what happened, when did she change, and where had our JayBear gone? Once I shared my concerns with Dr. Wilson, she began to have Jayla tested.

In early 2002, her test results confirmed that she was on the Autism spectrum. After her diagnosis, I began to relive the same torment that I experienced when she had her first operation at seven weeks old. I wondered if there was something that I possibly could have done differently. Could I have taken another brand of prenatal vitamins? Could I have eaten even more healthily? Could I have done anything at all to prevent her from being this way? I felt inadequate for giving my parents a granddaughter with Special Needs. I blamed myself for her having to undergo surgeries, therapy, and so many obstacles. I struggled with the heaviness of feeling like a disappointment to Jayla, my parents, and my family. It was taxing to accept the reality that Jayla's achievements would never be quite like her peers. I prayed so hard for understanding.

When I realized that her non-verbal symptom could be permanent after the tests confirmed her condition, my biggest concern was her inability to tell us everyday things. How would she let us know if she was cold, if someone was hurting her, or if she still was not full after eating breakfast, lunch, or dinner? My relentless apprehensions were a part of my daily thought process. No matter where I was or what I was doing: she was constantly at the forefront of my mind because she is my heart. And you know what? Some things never change because although she has overcome so much, she is still constantly on my mind because she will always be my heart.

That first autumn after her new diagnosis, I had a challenging day in October. We had just made it home from shopping for long-sleeved shirts, lightweight jackets, pants, and shoes. After I hung up her new clothes, I went into my room. I sat at the foot of my bed and cried. I was fighting back the tears the whole time I put her new outfits away because I wondered how I would decide to dress her every day. Was she hot-natured like my dad, brother, and me? Or was she super cold-natured like my mom? How would she let me know if she was not warm enough or if she was too hot? I asked God, *"Please help me take care of my baby."* Suddenly, Jayla dashed past my bedroom door with one of her new jackets draped around her neck and shoulders like a cape! I walked down the hall to get a closer look at her. She was clasping it tightly even though it was still on the hanger! My sadness instantly turned into laughter.

Actually, I even felt a glimmer of hope. I realized that God was showing me that although *she* was non-verbal, *He* would give her ways to let me know what she needed. I told my parents and friends what Jayla had done. We all laughed at our *"Supergirl."* I thanked God for quickly giving me a sign, calming me down with a good laugh, and swiftly answering my tearful prayer.

Dr. Wilson's staff, her neurosurgeon's staff, and I coordinated with her early intervention program manager to ensure that Jayla was enrolled in every type of therapy available to her. Unfortunately, the First Steps program would end when she turned three years old, so she only had a few months of eligibility. However, her therapists were fantastic. She made tremendous progress. They taught me so many skills to help reinforce their treatment sessions. My parents and brother learned new methods as well. I was immeasurably grateful that God was blessing her: life was good.

When we returned home from a trip to Louisiana in March 2006, Jayla had a high fever. She was agitated and fretful. Since she was non-verbal and had the VP shunt, we took her to the ER to be sure it was not anything serious. We did not then and still do not now take any chances with her health. When my mom & I took Jayla to the emergency room that evening, we had no idea she would spend approximately the next seven weeks in the hospital.

Who knew that she would develop four types of infection simultaneously? We would never have dreamed that she would spend her sixth birthday hemorrhaging from her brain with a clean-shaven head in the hospital. For weeks, an external shunt tube led from her head connected to a clear container next to her bed that forced us to constantly see the bloody fluid. Who would have thought that her organs would begin to shut down from intravenously taking three of the most potent antibiotics on the market concurrently? How could we have known that our family would celebrate that Easter and Mother's Day by taking turns at the hospital with our daughter, granddaughter, and niece? There was no way we could have anticipated Jayla needing two brain operations in less than two months, the countless needles, therapy to help her walk again, or our numerous sleepless nights due to us staring at her to make sure that she was still breathing because she was so frail.

Our entire biological family, close friends, church families, work friends, and friends from all across the country kept us covered in prayer. Several traveled across state lines to visit. They all called, texted, and showed us how much they cared. They never allowed us to question for even one second how much they loved us. We could see and feel God's answers to each and every prayer that was said for Jayla! I am still appreciative and always will be infinitely grateful.

Doctor Jesse and Evangelist Andrea Kelly were our religious leaders at the time. They both consistently called, visited Jayla, prayed with our family, and cared enough to introduce us to their sister-in-law, who was an excellent pediatrician in Nashville, Tennessee. She was extremely helpful during Jayla's extended hospital stay in Mississippi. She provided caring medical advice, various health suggestions, and most importantly, prayers via telephone. The expert questions that she had me to ask Jayla's medical team had them baffled. One of the residents told me that I asked *too many* questions. However, his opinion did not stop me from inquiring about every decision regarding her care. He told me that I gave them a run for their money. All I could do was smile and thank Jehovah Jireh for Dr. Kelly. She was our *ram in the bush*!

After Jayla's release from the hospital in Jackson, Dr. Kelly offered to provide further treatment and coordinated testing at Vanderbilt Hospital in Nashville. God knew *exactly* who we needed for this phase: the Bowie family graciously welcomed us into their home. Dr. Kelly and her staff provided extraordinary medical care. She and her family embraced us beyond the office as well. The Bowie and The Kelly families both showed us exceptional hospitality. Returning home was bittersweet, but it made the long trip worthwhile because Jayla's health remarkably improved.

***"We are home!"***

That was the thought that repeatedly ran through my mind as I fell across the couch on that beautiful summer day in June 2006. I had just given Jayla her afternoon medications. Afterwards, I decided to go into the living room since I had mostly been in bed the last two days after my seven-hour drive back to Mississippi from Tennessee. I ate a pre-packaged cup of all-natural applesauce because I did not have much of an appetite, but I knew my body needed some form of nourishment.

I was exhausted in every area ~ spiritually, mentally, physically, and emotionally. Although we were home, my anxiety was still in constant overdrive due to being her mom, advocate, social worker, nurse, caregiver, protector, and physical therapist. As I laid there, I thought, *"God, please help me rest."* I began making my requests known to Him by specifically stating what I needed in my prayer. {Philippians 4:6} A few hours passed, I watched a couple of sitcoms, and it was almost time for Jayla's next dose of medication. As I tried to convince myself to get up, I whispered again, *"Help, Lord!"* because I still felt excessively drained. However, Jayla needed me and I was certainly going to be there for her. Just as clear as the words you are reading right this moment, God began speaking to me, *"You do it! You establish an organization that embraces, encourages, and empowers Autism and Special Needs families. You offer support to other mothers, family members, and caregivers who are feeling just like you are right now. You provide the quality service you are searching for. You offer them hope."* At that precise moment, God granted me *Green Light Grace* as an Autism mom!

Have you ever been heading to work, a church service, a doctor's appointment, or an important meeting and you needed traffic to flow in perfect harmony in order to arrive on time? As you approach each intersection, you whisper a prayer to ask that the light synchronization works in your favor. You might even mentally cross your fingers, hoping that this small gesture will give your desperate prayer an express boost to Heaven so that God will answer speedily. I think we have all felt this way at least once, twice, or on numerous occasions in our lives.

In that particular instant on the couch, it was as if God allowed all the lights on my journey to turn *green* at the same time and absolutely *everything* made sense. My tears, fears, and years of feeling helpless, guilty, and confused were all preparing me to help others. God shifted me from my *broken mentality* into my *breakthrough mindset*! He lifted my head.

{Psalm 3:3} He supernaturally perfected my weaknesses with His strength. I perfectly understood how His grace had been sufficient for me in every situation Jayla and I faced. {2 Corinthians 12:8-10} I felt His peace that surpasses all understanding when I began to realize just how many times that He guarded my heart and kept my mind when I actually felt like falling apart.

{Philippians 4:7} He gave me another victory! {1 Corinthians 15:57} That revelation was my *Green Light Grace* moment.

Consequently, I am ecstatic about supporting individuals and their entire families affected by Autism and Special Needs. It is my desire for every parent, grandparent, sibling, extended family member, caregiver, educator, and all other roles connected to this community to experience the same liberation God gave me. However, my greatest passion is for mothers. I know exactly how it feels to be overexerted, overwhelmed, overcautious, overworked, and overlooked. Yet, even with the myriad of twists and turns, ups and downs, ins and outs, overs and unders, I know that God is with each of us who are connected to His uniquely designed individuals in *The G.U.D. Life* because *We Are Chosen*!

***"Yes, you will suffer for a short time. But after that, God will make everything right. He will make you strong. He will support you and keep you from falling. He is the God who gives all grace. He chose you to share in his glory in Christ. That glory will continue forever."***
***1 Peter 5:10 ERV***

**Shervondaline Sims Breedlove** was born and raised in Monroe, Louisiana. Her Grammy began calling her a natural- born leader before she even turned a year old. She is a Christian, Autism Advocate, Special Needs Champion, Author, Visionary Anthologist, Entrepreneur, Certified Master Life Coach, and Certified Spiritual Life Coach.

One of her most rewarding and fulfilling roles is being a caring mother to her only daughter, Jayla. Their journey is a true example of love, resilience, hope, healing, and strength. Their experiences are the fuel that ignites Shervondaline's passion and motivates her inspiration to provide assistance and benefits to other families affected by Autism and Special Needs. Being an Autism Advocate for twenty-one years has equipped Shervondaline with a profound level of compassion, significant knowledge of the effects on the entire family, and a broader understanding of social functioning impacts.

God blessed Shervondaline with the gift of encouragement and a giving heart. He has mantled her to bridge the gap for individuals and families affected by Autism and Special Needs by establishing a universal non-profit organization that provides an inclusive environment for support, growth, and total wellness. She knows that essential resources are vital for a victorious life. Shervondaline believes that people within this unique community are absolutely better together.

Shervondaline resides in Texas with her husband, Arthur, and their daughter, Jayla. She enjoys watching movies, reading, listening to music, traveling, and spending quality time with her family.

**Connect with Shervondaline**
Email: ssbreedlove220@gmail.com
Facebook: AuthorSSBreedlove
Instagram: AuthorSSBreedlove

## *"A Prayer For G.U.D. Babies and Children"*

### *John 14:13-14 NLT*

Heavenly Father, we humbly come to You in Jesus' Holy Name. {Matthew 18:18-20 KJV} We lift our babies and children to You in prayer. Lord, we want them to know You honestly. We ask that You allow them to walk in Your Presence. {Psalm 116:9 NLT} We ask that You grant them the opportunity to sense and know Your loving kindness and tender mercies daily. {Lamentations 3:22-24 KJV} We pray that they will desire to be in Your Presence all the days of their lives. Lord God, we ask You to saturate them in Your favor, anointing, and The Blood of Jesus. We petition You to draw them closer to You and all that you are.

Heavenly Father, we ask that they genuinely grow in the grace and knowledge of Who You Are. {2 Peter 3:18 NKJV} Lord, we love them deeply. We know that You love them more than we could ever possibly comprehend. We confidently trust You with our babies and children and every aspect of their lives now and always. You have given them wisdom and brilliance of their own, which is beyond our ability to understand. Abba Father, cover them with Your Blood as we commit them into Your Hands. Heavenly Father, we accept that You have set our babies and children apart for You only and whatever is pleasing in Your sight. Therefore, we ask You to always prepare a way for them.

Lord God, as parents, we ask You to bless our children with humility. {Philippians 2:3-4 NLT} We ask You to send Your angels to protect them, to watch over them, and to rebuke the devourer. Please shield them from evil and all darkness every day of their lives. Break all harmful and negative influences that are in or will come into their lives in Jesus' name. {Psalm 121:5-6 NLT}

Father, place their feet on Your path to walk and be with You forever. Lord, as parents, we dedicate our families to You. We ask You to help us to parent our uniquely designed children. Lord, help us to love them the way You love them! Help us speak words of love and encouragement, be there for and with them through life, and support and not tear down. We pray that You cause our words to be from You and go into their hearts and minds bringing forth life because we love them immensely. You have placed Your love in us to love them! We ask that they walk upright during their lives on Earth, in love with You, and without fear of man. {Proverbs 2:6-8 NIV} We pray that our babies and children will rejoice continually, grow into mighty prayer warriors, and always pray with thankful hearts. {1Thessalonians 5:16-18}

Thank You, we know that they will victoriously thrive because You are faithful! {1 Corinthians 15:57 NKJV} We believe it is so in the matchless name of our Lord Jesus Christ, Amen.

# *G.U.D. Daily Affirmations*

***Job 22:28***

1. I decree and declare that I love being a G.U.D. parent and teaching my child about God's love: this role brings me indescribable joy. {3 John 4 MSG}

2. I decree and declare that I am aware of my child's condition and I know that God equipped me to be a G.U.D. supportive parent. {Ephesians 2:10 AMP}

3. I decree and declare that I live a peaceful, positive, and prosperous G.U.D. life. {Romans 15:13 NLT}

4. I decree and declare that I patiently listen with my heart, understand what is needed, and provide G.U.D. solutions. {Ephesians 4:2-3 NIV}

5. I decree and declare that I take time for self-care, my health, and my personal needs. I know these activities support me being a G.U.D. parent. {Ecclesiastes 3:13 GNT}

6. I decree and declare that God has given me G.U.D. communication skills. {Ephesians 4:29 NLT}

7. I decree and declare that our home is a G.U.D. place of acceptance, security, joy, serenity, and unconditional love. {Proverbs 24:3-4 ESV}

8. I decree and declare that we will pray, seek God's answers, and allow Him to lead us to G.U.D. solutions that make a difference when something is out of balance. {Jeremiah 29:12-13 NIV}

9. I decree and declare that God will guide us to even greater G.U.D. in our lives. {Psalm 32:8 NIV}

10. I decree and declare that our family is fantastic and we always have a G.U.D. time when we are together. {Deuteronomy 26:11 NLT}

Made in USA - Crawfordsville, IN
63582_9780578992402
10.20.2021 1306